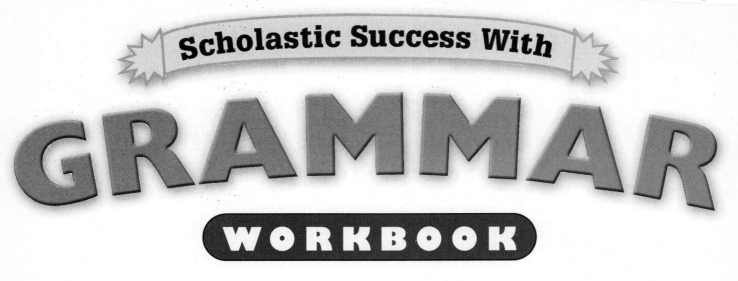

Scholastic Success With
GRAMMAR
WORKBOOK

GRADE 2

SCHOLASTIC
PROFESSIONAL BOOKS

New York • Toronto • London • Auckland • Sydney • Mexico City
New Delhi • Hong Kong • Buenos Aires

About the Book

"Nothing Succeeds Like Success."
—Alexandre Dumas the Elder, 1854

And no other resource boosts kids' grammar skills like *Scholastic Success With Grammar*! For classroom or at-home use, this exciting series for kids in grades 1 through 6 provides invaluable reinforcement and practice in grammar topics such as:

- sentence types
- parts of speech
- common and proper nouns
- sentence structure
- contractions
- verb tenses
- subject-verb agreement
- punctuation
- capitalization
  and more!

Each 64-page book contains loads of clever practice pages to keep kids challenged and excited as they strengthen the grammar skills they need to read and write well.

You'll also find lots of assessment sheets that give kids realistic practice in taking standardized tests – and help you see their progress!

What makes Scholastic Success With Grammar so solid?
Each practice page in the series reinforces a specific, age-appropriate skill as outlined in one or more of the following standardized tests:

- Iowa Tests of Basic Skills
- California Tests of Basic Skills
- California Achievement Test
- Metropolitan Achievement Test
- Stanford Achievement Test

Take the lead and help kids succeed with *Scholastic Success With Grammar*. Parents and teachers agree: No one helps kids succeed like Scholastic.

Table of Contents

ISBN: 0-439-43399-1

Telling Sentences and Questions

> A **telling sentence** tells something. It begins with a capital letter and ends with a period.
> A **question** asks something. It begins with a capital letter and ends with a question mark.

▶ Read each sentence. Write T on the line if the sentence is a telling sentence. Write Q on the line if it is a question.

1 I took my pet to see the vet. _____

2 Was your pet sick? _____

3 What did the vet do? _____

4 The vet checked my pet. _____

5 The vet said my pet had a cold. _____

▶ The order of the words in a sentence can change its meaning. Write *T* next to the sentence that is a telling sentence. Write Q next to the sentence that is a question.

6 Is your pet well now? _____

7 Now your pet is well. _____

Telling Sentences and Questions

> A **telling sentence** tells something. It begins with a capital letter and ends with a period.
> A **question** asks something. It begins with a capital letter and ends with a question mark.

▶ Underline the capital letter that begins each sentence. Add a period (.) if it is a telling sentence. Add a question mark (?) if it is a question.

1 The vet is nice _____

2 She helped my dog _____

3 Did she see your cat _____

4 Is the cat well now _____

5 My cat feels better _____

▶ The order of the words in a sentence can change its meaning. Change the word order in the telling sentence to make it a question. Write the question.

6 He will take the cat home.

_____

Telling Sentences and Questions

▶ Look at the underlined part of each sentence. If it is written correctly, fill in the last bubble. If not, fill in the bubble next to the correct answer.

1 The <u>girl</u> likes dogs.
- ⚪ the girl
- ⚪ Girl the
- ⚪ correct as is

2 <u>the vet</u> helps sick pets.
- ⚪ the Vet
- ⚪ The vet
- ⚪ correct as is

3 The boy likes <u>cats?</u>
- ⚪ cats.
- ⚪ cats
- ⚪ correct as is

4 Is the vet <u>nice?</u>
- ⚪ nice
- ⚪ nice.
- ⚪ correct as is

5 do <u>you</u> have a pet?
- ⚪ Do You
- ⚪ Do you
- ⚪ correct as is

6 <u>Is when</u> the vet open?
- ⚪ When is
- ⚪ when Is
- ⚪ correct as is

7 <u>he has</u> a bird.
- ⚪ Has he
- ⚪ He has
- ⚪ correct as is

8 My dog likes <u>the vet?</u>
- ⚪ The vet.
- ⚪ the vet.
- ⚪ correct as is

9 Who has a <u>goldfish.</u>
- ⚪ goldfish?
- ⚪ goldfish
- ⚪ correct as is

10 will <u>you</u> see the vet again?
- ⚪ Will you
- ⚪ You
- ⚪ correct as is

Exclamations and Commands

▶ Read each sentence. Write E if the sentence is an exclamation. Write C if the sentence is a command.

1 Ruby copies Angela! ——

2 Look at their dresses. ——

3 They're exactly the same! ——

4 Angela is mad! ——

5 Look at Ruby! ——

6 Show Angela how Ruby hops. ——

▶ Write each sentence correctly.

Exclamation be yourself

7 _____

Command don't copy other people

8 _____

Exclamations and Commands

▶ Read each exclamation. Use words from the box to tell what strong feeling it shows.

> An **exclamation** shows strong feelings, such as excitement, surprise, or fear. It begins with a capital letter and ends with an exclamation mark (!).
> A **command** makes a request or tells someone to do something. It ends with a period or an exclamation mark.

| excitement | fear | anger | surprise |

1 I lost my jacket. I'll be so cold! _____

2 Look what I have! _____

3 I didn't know you had my jacket! _____

4 Give it to me now! _____

▶ Look at the picture.

5 Circle the command that goes with the picture.

Please don't be upset!   Wear your new hat.

6 Write another command for the picture.

_____

7 Write an exclamation for the picture.

_____

Exclamations and Commands

▶ Read each exclamation. If it is written correctly, fill in the last bubble. If not, fill in the bubble next to the correct way to write it.

1 You are a great hopper
- ○ you are a great hopper!
- ○ you are a great hopper.
- ○ You are a great hopper!
- ○ correct as is

2 the picture looks beautiful.
- ○ The picture looks beautiful!
- ○ The picture looks beautiful
- ○ the picture looks beautiful!
- ○ correct as is

3 i can paint, too!
- ○ i can paint, too
- ○ I can paint, too!
- ○ I can paint, too
- ○ correct as is

4 I did it!
- ○ i did it!
- ○ I did it
- ○ i did it
- ○ correct as is

▶ Read each command. If it is written correctly, fill in the last bubble. If not, fill in the bubble next to the correct way to write it.

5 teach me how to hop.
- ○ teach me how to hop
- ○ Teach me how to hop
- ○ Teach me how to hop.
- ○ correct as is

6 Hop backward like this
- ○ Hop backward like this.
- ○ hop backward like this
- ○ hop backward like this!
- ○ correct as is

Types of Sentences; Capital *I*

▶ Read each sentence. Circle the beginning letter, end punctuation, and the word I in each sentence.

1 I sail my boat in the lake.

2 May I have a turn?

3 I am so happy!

4 Can Kiku and I play?

5 Bill and I fly the kite.

A **telling sentence** begins with a capital letter and ends with a period. A **question** begins with a capital letter and ends with a question mark. An **exclamation** begins with a capital letter and ends with an exclamation mark. A **command** begins with a capital letter and ends with a period. The word *I* is always capitalized in a sentence.

▶ Write each sentence in the correct box.

Telling Sentences

_____

_____

Questions

_____

_____

Exclamation _____

Types of Sentences; Capital *I*

▶ Decide if each sentence is a telling sentence, a question, an exclamation, or a command. Write *T, Q, E,* or C on the lines.

> A **telling sentence** begins with a capital letter and ends with a period. A **question** begins with a capital letter and ends with a question mark. An **exclamation** begins with a capital letter and ends with an exclamation mark. A **command** begins with a capital letter and ends with a period. The word *I* is always capitalized in a sentence.

1 My sister and I went to the lake. ____

2 Come see this. ____

3 I saw three little sailboats. ____

4 Put the boat in the water. ____

5 Did I have a good time? ____

6 You bet! I loved it! ____

7 Can I go again soon? ____

▶ What would you do at the lake? Use the word I and your own ideas to finish the sentences.

8 At the lake ____ saw _____ .

9 ____ can _____ .

10 My friend and ____ liked _____ best.

Types of Sentences; Capital *I*

▶ Read each sentence. If it is written correctly, fill in the last bubble.
If not, fill in the bubble next to the correct way to write it.

1 i have fun with my bike.

○ I have fun with my bike.
○ I have fun with my bike
○ i have fun with my bike
○ correct as is

2 can I ride to the beach

○ Can I ride to the beach
○ Can I ride to the beach?
○ Can i ride to the beach?
○ correct as is

3 i find a pretty shell

○ I find a pretty shell
○ i find a pretty shell.
○ I find a pretty shell.
○ correct as is

4 Jill and I see a crab.

○ Jill and I see a crab
○ Jill and i see a crab.
○ Jill and i see a crab
○ correct as is

5 get the shovel

○ Get the shovel
○ Get the shovel.
○ get the shovel.
○ correct as is

6 what a mess I made

○ What a mess I made!
○ What a mess I made
○ what a mess I made!
○ correct as is

Common Nouns

▶ Read each sentence. Circle the common nouns.

1 The boy made a boat.

2 The brothers went to the park.

3 A girl was with her grandmother.

4 Two boats crashed in the lake.

5 Friends used a needle and thread to fix the sail.

▶ Write the common nouns you circled under the correct heading below.

People	Places	Things
_____	_____	_____
_____	_____	_____
_____		_____
_____		_____

Common Nouns

Common nouns
name people, places,
or things.

▶ Help sort the cards. Some of the words
are nouns. Some are not. Circle the nouns.

▶ Write each noun you circled under the correct heading.

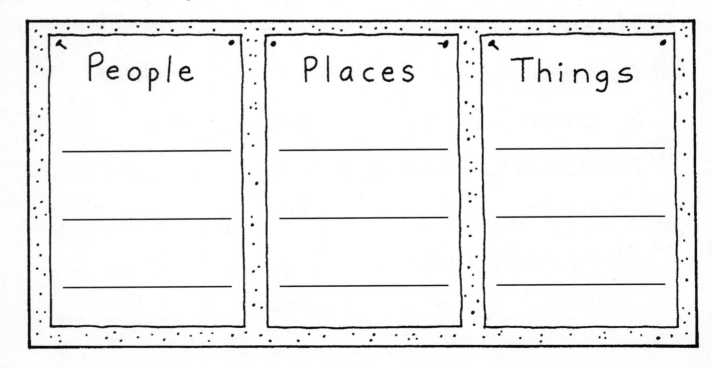

People   Places   Things

Common Nouns

▶ Look at the underlined word in each sentence. If it is a common noun, fill in the bubble next to yes. If it is not a common noun, fill in the bubble next to no.

1 Our class <u>went</u> on a trip.

  ◯ yes   ◯ no

2 We went to the <u>city</u>.

  ◯ yes   ◯ no

3 The buildings were <u>tall</u>.

  ◯ yes   ◯ no

4 There were many <u>cars</u>.

  ◯ yes   ◯ no

▶ A common noun is underlined in each sentence. Tell if it names a person, place or thing. Fill in the bubble next to the correct answer.

5 We went into a big <u>room</u>.

  ◯ person   ◯ place   ◯ thing

6 Our <u>teacher</u> led us.

  ◯ person   ◯ place   ◯ thing

7 I walked with my best <u>friend</u>.

  ◯ person   ◯ place   ◯ thing

8 We sat at a long <u>table</u>.

  ◯ person   ◯ place   ◯ thing

Capitalize Names and Places

> Special names of people and places always begin with capital letters. They are called **proper nouns.**

▶ Read each sentence. Circle the proper noun.

1 George Ancona is a photographer.

2 He was born in Mexico.

3 His family called him Jorgito.

4 They lived in Coney Island.

5 Now he travels to Honduras to take pictures.

6 Tio Mario worked in a sign shop.

▶ Write the proper nouns you circled under the correct heading below.

People

_____

_____

_____

Places

_____

_____

_____

Capitalize Names and Places

▶ Read the postcard. Find the proper nouns. Write them correctly on the lines below.

Dear sue,

It's very hot here in california. We visited the city of los angeles. Then we swam in the pacific ocean. I miss you.

Love,
tonya

sue wong
11 shore road
austin, texas 78728

1 _____

2 _____

3 _____

4 _____

5 _____

6 _____

7 _____

8 _____

▶ Write a sentence with a proper noun. Underline the capital letter or letters in the proper noun. Then write whether it names a person or a place.

_____

_____

Name

Capitalize Names and Places

▶ A proper noun is underlined in each sentence. Does it name a person or a place? Fill in the bubble next to the correct answer.

1 <u>Betty</u> is a photographer.

○ person ○ place

2 She goes to <u>Florida</u> to take pictures.

○ person ○ place

3 She meets her older brother <u>Peter</u>.

○ person ○ place

4 She takes his picture in a city called <u>Miami</u>.

○ person ○ place

▶ Read each sentence. Find the proper noun. Fill in the bubble next to the word that is a proper noun.

5 Their friend is Emilio.

○ friend ○ Emilio

○ Their ○ is

6 They all went to Orlando.

○ Orlando ○ all

○ They ○ went

7 They visited Disney World there.

○ They

○ there

○ visited

○ Disney World

8 They walked down Main Street in the park.

○ park

○ walked

○ They

○ Main Street

Verbs

A **verb** is an action word. It tells what someone or something is doing.

▶ Read each sentence. Write the action verb in the telling part of the sentence.

1 Ronald runs to the field. _____

2 Michael wears a batting helmet. _____

3 He smacks the ball hard. _____

4 Ronald holds the wrong end of the bat. _____

5 He misses the ball. _____

6 Ronald waits in left field. _____

7 He writes G for great. _____

8 Ronald's father helps him. _____

▶ Write a sentence about the picture. Use an action verb and circle it.

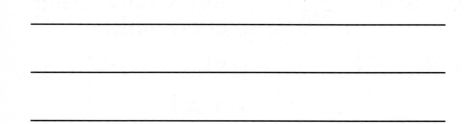

Verbs

▶ Draw a line to match each sentence with an action verb. Then write the action verbs on the lines to finish the sentences.

1 Moms and dads _____ the game.   throws

2 The pitcher _____ the ball.   opens

3 Ronald _____ his eyes.   watch

4 The team _____ for Ronald.   cheers

5 Ronald _____ the ball past the pitcher.   runs

6 He _____ to first base.   hits

7 Someone _____, "Go Ronald go!"   eat

8 The kids _____ ice cream after the game.   yells

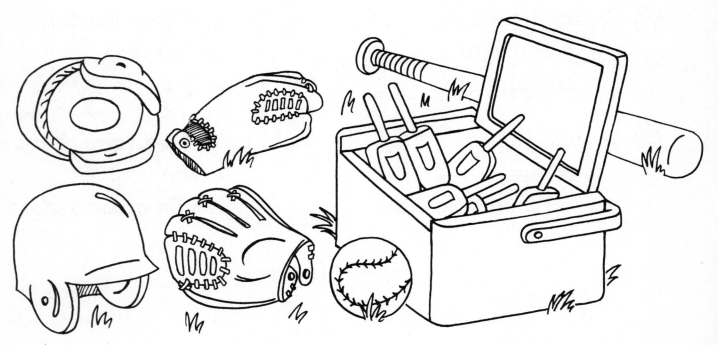

Verbs

▶ Look at the underlined word in each sentence. Fill in the correct bubble to tell whether or not it is an action verb.

1 The dog <u>runs</u> down the road.
- ◯ action verb
- ◯ not an action verb

2 The girl chases the <u>dog</u>.
- ◯ action verb
- ◯ not an action verb

3 The dog finds a <u>bone</u>.
- ◯ action verb
- ◯ not an action verb

4 The <u>sun</u> sets.
- ◯ action verb
- ◯ not an action verb

5 Rain <u>falls</u> from the sky.
- ◯ action verb
- ◯ not an action verb

6 The girl <u>splashes</u> water.
- ◯ action verb
- ◯ not an action verb

7 The dog hides <u>under</u> a bush.
- ◯ action verb
- ◯ not an action verb

8 The girl <u>finds</u> the dog.
- ◯ action verb
- ◯ not an action verb

9 The sun <u>shines</u>.
- ◯ action verb
- ◯ not an action verb

10 The girl sees a <u>rainbow</u>.
- ◯ action verb
- ◯ not an action verb

Simple Sentences

> A **simple sentence** has a naming part and a telling part. It tells a complete thought.

▶ Read each group of words. Put an X next to it if it is a complete thought. Circle the naming part and underline the telling part in each sentence.

1 One day thirsty _____

2 Crow could not get a drink. _____

3 The water rose. _____

4 The old mouse _____

5 Put the bell _____

6 One mouse had a plan. _____

▶ Write a simple sentence about the picture below. Circle the naming part and underline the telling part.

_____

Simple Sentences

> A **simple sentence** has a naming part and a telling part. It tells a complete thought.

▶ Circle the sentence in each pair. Then underline the naming part of the sentence.

1 (a) Lin likes to play soccer.

   (b) likes to play soccer

2 (a) Her friends

   (b) Her friends watch her play.

3 (a) They cheer for Lin.

   (b) They cheer for

4 (a) Her mom goes to all of her games.

   (b) goes to all of her games

5 (a) The coach is very proud of Lin.

   (b) The coach is

Simple Sentences

▶ Read each sentence. Fill in the bubble to tell if the underlined words are the naming or the telling part of the sentence. Some of the underlined words may not be the whole part.

1 The cat <u>was under the tree.</u>
- ○ naming part
- ○ telling part
- ○ not the whole part

2 <u>A bird</u> saw the cat.
- ○ naming part
- ○ telling part
- ○ not the whole part

3 The bird <u>flew</u> away.
- ○ naming part
- ○ telling part
- ○ not the whole part

4 <u>Then, the</u> cat walked away.
- ○ naming part
- ○ telling part
- ○ not the whole part

▶ Fill in the bubble to choose a naming or telling part that makes a sentence.

5 The bird ____.
- ○ in the tall tree
- ○ saw the cat go away
- ○ flying very fast in the sky

6 ____ came back to the tree.
- ○ Deep in the woods
- ○ The large and pretty
- ○ Then the bird

7 ____ saw the bird.
- ○ After a minute, the cat
- ○ Running across the grass
- ○ The cat was watching

8 So the cat ____.
- ○ walking to the tree
- ○ under the tree
- ○ walked back, too

Past-Tense Verbs

▶ Find the past-tense verb in each sentence. Write it on the line.

1 Last spring, Daisy planted a garden. _____

2 Floyd watered the garden. _____

3 Together they weeded their garden. _____

4 One day they discovered a big carrot. _____

▶ Read each sentence. If the sentence has a past-tense verb, write it on the line. If the sentence does not have a past-tense verb, leave the line blank.

5 They like to eat carrots. _____

6 They pulled on the carrot. _____

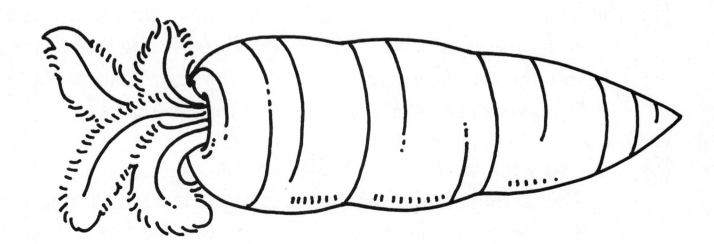

Name _____

Past-Tense Verbs

▶ Read the first sentence in each pair. Change the underlined verb to tell about the past.

1 Today my dogs <u>push</u> open the back door.

Yesterday my dogs _____ open the back door.

2 Today they <u>splash</u> in the rain puddles.

Last night they _____ in the rain puddles.

3 Now they <u>roll</u> in the mud.

Last week they _____ in the mud.

4 Today I <u>follow</u> my dogs' footprints.

Last Sunday I _____ my dogs' footprints.

5 Now I <u>wash</u> my dogs from head to toe.

Earlier I _____ my dogs from head to toe.

▶ Write a sentence using one of the verbs you wrote.

_____

_____

_____

Past-Tense Verbs

▶ Read each sentence. Look at the underlined verb. If it is
not correct, fill in the bubble next to the correct verb.
If it is correct, fill in the last bubble.

1 Last Saturday I <u>visit</u> John
in the country.
- ○ visited
- ○ correct as is

2 Two weeks ago we
<u>watched</u> a sailboat race.
- ○ watch
- ○ correct as is

3 A week ago we <u>walked</u> to
the top of a big hill.
- ○ walk
- ○ correct as is

4 Last week I <u>talk</u> to John on
the phone.
- ○ talked
- ○ correct as is

5 Earlier I <u>ask</u> him to visit me
in the city.
- ○ asked
- ○ correct as is

6 Friday morning his train
<u>pulled</u> into the station.
- ○ pull
- ○ correct as is

7 Last night my dog <u>barked</u>
when he saw John.
- ○ bark
- ○ correct as is

8 Yesterday I <u>show</u> John
around the city.
- ○ showed
- ○ correct as is

Pronouns

> Read each pair of sentences. Circle the
> pronoun in the second sentence of each pair.
> Then write what the pronoun stands for.
> The first one has been done for you.

A **pronoun** takes the place of the name of a person, place, or thing.

1 Wendell did not like to clean his room.

(He) liked a messy room.

_____Wendell_____

2 Mother wanted Wendell to do some work.

She handed Wendell a broom.

_____

3 The pigs came into Wendell's room.

They helped Wendell clean the room.

_____

4 Wendell and the pigs played a board game.

Wendell and the pigs had fun playing it.

_____

5 The pigs and Wendell played for a long time.

They liked to play games.

_____

6 Wendell was sad to see his friends go.

He liked playing with the pigs.

_____

Pronouns

> A **pronoun** takes the place of the name of a person, place, or thing.

▶ Read the story. Use the pronouns in the box to complete each sentence. The first one has been done for you.

| they | he | she | it |

Glenda was walking in the woods. At last ____she____ came to a house. _____ was empty. She opened the

1

door and saw three chairs by the fireplace. _____

2

were all different sizes. She sat down on the smallest one.

_____ was the perfect size for her. Soon _____

3   4

fell asleep. When she woke up, three pigs were

standing over her. The father pig spoke. _____

5

asked Glenda if she would stay for dinner. "I would love

to!" said Glenda.

Pronouns

▶ Read each sentence. Fill in the bubble next to the word or words that the underlined pronoun stands for.

1 <u>She</u> did not like the mess.
- ○ Wendell
- ○ The boy
- ○ The pigs
- ○ Mrs. Fultz

2 <u>He</u> did not like brooms.
- ○ The pigs
- ○ The boys
- ○ The boy
- ○ Mrs. Fultz

3 <u>It</u> was full of pigs.
- ○ The rooms
- ○ The house
- ○ The pigs
- ○ The door

4 <u>They</u> wanted to play.
- ○ The room
- ○ Wendell
- ○ The pigs
- ○ Mrs. Fultz

▶ Read each sentence. Fill in the bubble next to the pronoun that can take the place of the underlined word or words.

5 <u>Wendell</u> waved goodbye to the pigs.
- ○ He
- ○ She
- ○ It
- ○ They

6 Wendell hoped <u>the pigs</u> would come back.
- ○ it
- ○ he
- ○ they
- ○ she

Types of Sentences

▶ Read each sentence. Write it next to the correct heading.

> A **telling sentence** tells something. A **question** asks something. An **exclamation** shows strong feelings. A **command** makes a request or gives a command.

What a big mango!   I like mangos.

Is that a banana?   Did you find the fruit?

Buy me an avocado.   Come over for dinner.

I want to eat dinner.   This tastes great!

Exclamation: _____

_____

Command: _____

_____

Question: _____

_____

Telling Sentence: _____

_____

Types of Sentences

▶ Read the following sentences. Write the correct end punctuation mark for each sentence. Then write the sentence type on the line to the right of each sentence. Write **T** for each telling sentence or statement, **Q** for each question, **E** for each exclamation, and **C** for each command.

> A **telling sentence** tells something. A **question** asks something. An **exclamation** shows strong feelings. A **command** makes a request or gives a command.

1 We're going to the beach __ _____

2 Do you have your bathing suit __ _____

3 We will play in the sand __ _____

4 Pack the sunscreen __ _____

5 I love swimming __ _____

6 Take the beach chair __ _____

7 What time do we leave __ _____

8 Wow, that's a huge wave __ _____

Types of Sentences

▶ Read each sentence. Fill in the bubble next to the correct type of sentence.

1 Give me that apple.
○ telling ○ question ○ exclamation ○ command

2 What kind of fruit is this?
○ telling ○ question ○ exclamation ○ command

3 What a great dinner!
○ telling ○ question ○ exclamation ○ command

4 Buy this watermelon.
○ telling ○ question ○ exclamation ○ command

5 This is the best watermelon!
○ telling ○ question ○ exclamation ○ command

6 I would like to have another piece.
○ telling ○ question ○ exclamation ○ command

7 Are those bananas ripe?
○ telling ○ question ○ exclamation ○ command

8 A mango is smaller than a watermelon.
○ telling ○ question ○ exclamation ○ command

Word Order

▶ Read each group of words. Write the words in the correct order to make a statement. Begin each statement with a capital letter and end it with a period.

1 brothers two can live together

_____

2 Hungbu find will a home new

_____

3 will fix Mother the house

_____

▶ Read each group of words. Write the words in the correct order to make a question. Begin each question with a capital letter and end it with a question mark.

4 clean Sister will house the

_____

5 help can the bird them

_____

Word Order

▶ Write the words in the correct order to make a sentence. Then write if the sentence is a question or a statement.

1 find Will I some wood? _____

_____

2 must Each of help us. _____

_____

3 trees are the Where? _____

_____

▶ Write each group of words in the correct order to make a statement. Then write them in the correct order to make a question. Add capital letters and end punctuation to your sentences.

4 your pumpkin is that _____

_____

5 help cut you can pumpkin the _____

_____

Word Order

▶ Read each group of words. If the word order does not make sense, fill in the bubble next to the correct word order. If the words are in an order that makes sense, fill in the last bubble.

1 Dad made breakfast for eggs.
- ○ Made for breakfast Dad eggs.
- ○ Dad made breakfast eggs for.
- ○ Dad made eggs for breakfast.
- ○ correct as is

2 Open eggs four he cracked.
- ○ He cracked eggs open four.
- ○ He cracked open four eggs.
- ○ Four eggs cracked open he.
- ○ correct as is

3 Like do eggs you?
- ○ Eggs do you like?
- ○ Do you like eggs?
- ○ Do eggs like you?
- ○ correct as is

4 Help did you him?
- ○ Did help you him?
- ○ Did you help him?
- ○ Help you did him?
- ○ correct as is

5 With fork a beat eggs.
- ○ Beat eggs with a fork.
- ○ Eggs beat a fork with.
- ○ A fork beat with eggs.
- ○ correct as is

6 Do you want some toast?
- ○ Do you toast some want?
- ○ Do some toast want you?
- ○ You want do some toast?
- ○ correct as is

Plural Nouns

▶ Read the sentences. Underline the plural nouns. Circle the letter or letters that were added to mean more than one.

1 We have two accordions in our house.

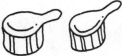

2 Grandma has many brushes to fix her hair.

3 My grandfather has many clocks and watches.

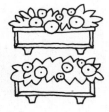

4 A lot of flowers are in the boxes.

▶ Write the nouns that add -s.

_____

▶ Write the nouns that add -es.

_____

Plural Nouns

Most nouns add **-s** to mean more than one. Nouns that end in **s**, **x**, **ch**, or **sh** add **-es** to mean more than one.

▶ Read each sentence. Add -s or -es to the noun at the end of the sentence to make it plural. Write it in the sentence.

1 Dad made five cheese _____. (sandwich)

2 He packed five _____ for the children. (lunch)

3 Lisa put fruit in all the _____. (lunchbox)

4 She packed some paper _____, **too.** (dish)

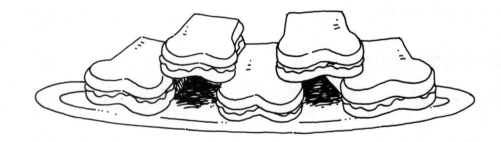

▶ Write the plural for each noun on the line.

5 one box

two _____

6 one dress

two _____

7 one coat

two _____

8 one bench

two _____

Plural Nouns

▶ Read each pair of nouns. If the plural noun is correct, fill
in the last bubble. If it is not correct, fill in the bubble next
to the correct plural noun.

1 sketch, sketchs

　　◯ sketches

　　◯ correct as is

2 tree, trees

　　◯ treess

　　◯ correct as is

3 fox, foxs

　　◯ foxes

　　◯ correct as is

4 paint, paints

　　◯ paintes

　　◯ correct as is

5 squirrel, squirrels

　　◯ squirreles

　　◯ correct as is

6 dress, dressees

　　◯ dresses

　　◯ correct as is

7 ball, balles

　　◯ balls

　　◯ correct as is

8 wish, wishes

　　◯ wishs

　　◯ correct as is

Adjectives

▶ Read each sentence. Underline the nouns. Write the adjective that tells about each noun.

1 The brown donkey carried the heavy sack.

_____ _____

2 The striped cat chased two birds.

_____ _____

3 The little rooster crowed six times.

_____ _____

▶ Write the adjectives from the sentences above.

4 Write the adjectives that tell what kind.

_____

5 Write the adjectives that tell how many.

_____

Adjectives

▶ Read each sentence. Find the adjective and the noun it describes. Circle the noun. Write the adjective on the line.

1 Peggy and Rosa went to the big zoo. _____

2 They looked up at the tall giraffe. _____

3 The giraffe looked down at the two girls. _____

4 The giraffe had brown spots. _____

▶ Write adjectives from the sentences in the chart.

Color Word	Size Words	Number Word
_____	_____	_____
	_____	

Adjectives

▶ Read each sentence. Fill in the bubble next to the word that is an adjective.

1 In the morning, Jenny put on red boots.

○ put   ○ boots

○ red   ○ on

2 She found a yellow hat in the closet.

○ She   ○ hat

○ found   ○ yellow

3 She opened her purple umbrella.

○ opened   ○ She

○ umbrella   ○ purple

4 Jenny walked past a big house.

○ big   ○ house

○ walked   ○ past

5 She waved to three friends.

○ waved   ○ three

○ to   ○ friends

6 A little puppy trotted behind her.

○ trotted   ○ puppy

○ little   ○ behind

7 She jumped over a huge puddle.

○ She   ○ jumped

○ huge   ○ puddle

8 Two birds took a drink of water.

○ birds   ○ of

○ took   ○ Two

Verb *to be*

Am, is, are, was, and were are forms of the verb to be. These verbs show being instead of action.

▶ Read each sentence. Underline the verb. Write *past* if the sentence tells about the past. Write *now* if the sentence tells about the present.

1 The story is perfect.

_____

2 The producers are happy.

_____

3 The actors were funny.

_____

4 The movie studio is interested in the story.

_____

5 I am excited about the movie.

_____

6 I was sad at the end.

_____

Verb *to be*

▶ Choose a verb from the box to finish each sentence. There may be more than one right answer. Write *one* if the sentence tells about one. Write *more* if it tells about more than one.

> am   is   are   was   were

1 The movie _____ long. _____

2 She _____ in the movie. _____

3 They _____ at the movie theater yesterday. _____

4 The producers _____ spending money now. _____

5 The director _____ not at work yesterday. _____

6 The actors _____ acting now. _____

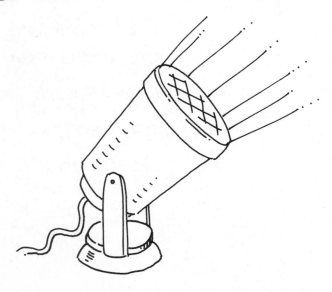 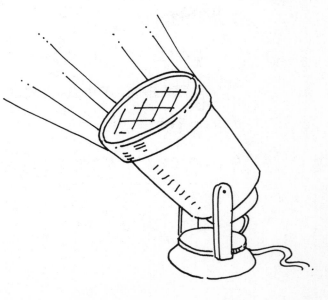

Name

Verb *to be*

▶ Read each sentence. Fill in the bubble next to the words that correctly tell about the sentence.

1 The movie was very long.
- ○ past, more than one
- ○ present, more than one
- ○ past, one
- ○ present, one

2 The seats at the movies are high up.
- ○ past, more than one
- ○ present, more than one
- ○ past, one
- ○ present, one

3 The actors were all big stars.
- ○ past, more than one
- ○ present, more than one
- ○ past, one
- ○ present, one

4 The scenes were interesting.
- ○ past, more than one
- ○ present, more than one
- ○ past, one
- ○ present, one

5 The trees and flowers were so beautiful.
- ○ past, more than one
- ○ present, more than one
- ○ past, one
- ○ present, one

6 I am going to see the movie again.
- ○ past, more than one
- ○ present, more than one
- ○ past, one
- ○ present, one

Irregular Verbs
go, do

▶ Read each sentence. Write present if the underlined verb tells about action now. Write past if it tells about action in the past.

Present	Past
go, goes	went
do, does	did

1 Grace <u>goes</u> to the playground. _____

2 Some other children <u>go</u>, too. _____

3 Grace <u>does</u> a scene from a story. _____

4 The children <u>do</u> the scene with her. _____

5 Grace <u>went</u> into battle as Joan of Arc. _____

6 She <u>did</u> the part of Anansi the Spider, too. _____

7 In another part, Grace <u>went</u> inside a
wooden horse. _____

8 She <u>did</u> many other parts. _____

Irregular Verbs
go, do

▶ Choose the correct word from the chart and write it on the line.

In the Present	In the Past
go, goes	went
do, does	did

Irregular verbs change their spelling when they tell about the past.

Did is the past form of **do** and **does**.

Went is the past form of **go** and **goes**.

1 Last week our family _____ to the art museum.

2 Pablo _____ there a lot.

3 His mother _____ the displays there now.

4 She _____ a new one yesterday.

5 _____ you want to join us tomorrow?

6 We want to _____ after lunch again.

Irregular Verbs *go, do*

▶ Fill in the bubble next to the word that correctly completes the sentence.

1 Rose ____ to the ballet.
- ◯ go
- ◯ did
- ◯ goes

2 Two dancers ____ a kick and a turn.
- ◯ do
- ◯ does
- ◯ goes

3 Another dancer ____ a hop and a jump.
- ◯ went
- ◯ does
- ◯ do

4 They ____ around in circles very fast.
- ◯ goes
- ◯ did
- ◯ go

5 A girl ____ two big splits.
- ◯ do
- ◯ did
- ◯ went

6 Then she ____ off stage.
- ◯ go
- ◯ did
- ◯ went

7 Rose ____ home feeling very happy.
- ◯ went
- ◯ did
- ◯ go

8 She ____ some of the steps, too.
- ◯ do
- ◯ did
- ◯ goes

Quotation Marks

▶ Read each sentence. Underline the exact words the speaker says. Put the words in quotation marks. The first one is done for you.

Quotation marks show the exact words someone says. They go before the speaker's first word. They also go after the speaker's last word and the end punctuation mark.

1 Max said, "Let's go on a picnic."

2 Cori replied,   That's a great idea.

3 Andy asked,   What should we bring?

4 Max said with a laugh,   We should bring food.

5 Cori added,   Yes, let's bring lots and lots of food.

6 Andy giggled and said,   You're no help at all!

▶ Finish the sentences below by writing what Max, Cori, and Andy might say next. Use quotation marks.

7 Max said, _____.

8 Cori asked, _____.

9 Andy answered, _____.

Quotation Marks

▶ Read the sentences. Then put quotation marks where they belong. The first one has been done for you.

> **Quotation marks** show the exact words someone says. They go before the speaker's first word. They also go after the speaker's last word and the end punctuation mark.

1 Jan cried, "It is raining!"

2 She asked,   What will we do today?

3 Tomas answered,   We could read.

4 Tomas whispered,   Maybe the sun will come out soon.

5 Jan whined,   But what will we do now?

6 Tomas said,   Use your imagination!

▶ Finish the sentence below. Use quotation marks to show what Jan asked.

Jan asked, _____

_____

Quotation Marks

Fill in the bubble next to the correct way to write the sentence.

1

○ Let's make a sand castle, said Lenny.

○ "Let's make a sand castle, said Lenny.

○ "Let's make a sand castle," said Lenny.

2

○ Where's the pail and shovel?" asked Sonya.

○ "Where's the pail and shovel?" asked Sonya.

○ Where's the pail and shovel? asked Sonya

3

○ Sara said, "Maybe Otis can help."

○ Sara said, Maybe Otis can help."

○ Sara said, "Maybe Otis can help.

4

○ Do you want to dig? asked Lenny.

○ "Do you want to dig? asked Lenny.

○ "Do you want to dig?" asked Lenny.

5

○ Sonya shouted, Get some water!

○ Sonya shouted, "Get some water!

○ Sonya shouted, "Get some water!"

6

○ Look what we made! cried the children.

○ "Look what we made!" cried the children.

○ Look what we made!" cried the children.

Contractions With *not*

> Read each sentence. Underline the contraction. Write the two words the contraction is made from.

A **contraction** is two words made into one word. An apostrophe takes the place of the missing letter or letters. In a contraction, **not** becomes **n't**.

1 The little old man and little old woman aren't ready. _____

2 The Gingerbread Man doesn't want to be eaten. _____

3 They can't catch him. _____

4 They couldn't run fast enough. _____

5 He didn't come back. _____

6 The Gingerbread Man isn't afraid of the fox. _____

> Draw a line to match each contraction to the two words it is made from.

7 hadn't   were not

8 don't   had not

9 weren't   do not

Contractions With *not*

► Read each sentence. Write a contraction for the underlined words.

> A **contraction** is two words made into one word. An apostrophe takes the place of the missing letter or letters. In a contraction, **not** becomes **n't**.

  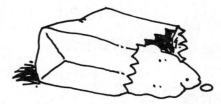

1 Cindy and Ed <u>could not</u> bake a cake. _____

2 There <u>was not</u> enough flour. _____

3 They <u>are not</u> happy. _____

4 They <u>cannot</u> surprise José. _____

5 <u>Do not</u> give up. _____

6 They <u>did not</u> give up.
They made cupcakes! _____

► Write a sentence using a contraction you wrote.

_____

_____

Contractions With *not*

▶ Fill in the bubble next to the contraction that correctly completes the sentence.

1 Our players ____ as big as theirs.
- ◯ doesn't
- ◯ haven't
- ◯ aren't

2 Our coach ____ worried.
- ◯ isn't
- ◯ didn't
- ◯ can't

3 They ____ run as fast as we can.
- ◯ weren't
- ◯ can't
- ◯ wasn't

4 Their runner ____ tag first base.
- ◯ doesn't
- ◯ haven't
- ◯ isn't

5 Their hitters ____ hit the ball hard.
- ◯ isn't
- ◯ weren't
- ◯ don't

6 Our hitters ____ miss any balls.
- ◯ doesn't
- ◯ didn't
- ◯ aren't

7 The other players ____ catch our balls.
- ◯ couldn't
- ◯ haven't
- ◯ isn't

8 They ____ ready for us.
- ◯ don't
- ◯ hadn't
- ◯ weren't

Subject/Verb Agreement

▶ Read each sentence. Underline the word in parentheses ( ) that correctly completes it. Write the word on the line.

If the naming part of a sentence names one, add **-s** to the action word. If the naming part names more than one, do not add **-s** to the action word.

1 Kim _____ a story about a monkey. (write, writes)

2 The monkey _____ his friend in the city. (meet, meets)

3 The two friends _____ on the bus. (ride, rides)

4 The monkeys _____ for toys and presents. (shop, shops)

5 The store _____ at 7 o'clock. (close, closes)

6 The monkeys _____ the time. (forget, forgets)

7 The owner _____ the door. (lock, locks)

8 The friends _____ on the window. (bang, bangs)

9 Many people _____ for help. (call, calls)

10 Finally the monkeys _____ the door open. (hear, hears)

Subject/Verb Agreement

▶ Read each sentence. Circle the action word in parentheses ( ) that correctly completes the sentence.

1 Two baby llamas (play/plays) in the mountains.

2 One baby llama (hide/hides) under a bush.

3 The baby animals (chase/chases) flying leaves.

4 Soon the mother llama (call/calls) them.

5 The babies (run/runs) to her.

6 The two babies (stand/stands) next to their mother.

7 One baby (close/closes) its eyes.

8 The mother llama (nudge/nudges) the baby gently.

9 But the baby llama (sleep/sleeps).

10 Soon both baby llamas (sleep/sleeps).

Subject/Verb Agreement

▶ Fill in the bubble next to the word that correctly completes the sentence.

1 Two friends ____ beautiful bead necklaces.
○ make   ○ makes

2 One girl ____ some pieces of string.
○ cut   ○ cuts

3 The girls ____ red, blue, and yellow beads.
○ use   ○ uses

4 The yellow beads ____ in the dark.
○ glow   ○ glows

5 The necklaces ____ from the rod.
○ hang   ○ hangs

6 The boys ____ a necklace for their mother.
○ buy   ○ buys

7 One boy ____ the short necklace with round beads.
○ pick   ○ picks

8 The other boy ____ the necklace with square beads.
○ pick   ○ picks

9 Two sisters ____ the same red necklace.
○ wear   ○ wears

10 The girls ____ all the necklaces.
○ sell   ○ sells

More About Subject/Verb Agreement

▶ Read each sentence. Circle the correct verb to complete it.

1 John and his family (camp, camps) in the woods.

2 Alice (like, likes) hiking the best.

3 John (walk, walks) ahead of everyone.

4 Mom and John (build, builds) a campfire.

5 Dad and Alice (cook, cooks) dinner over the fire.

6 Alice and Mom (crawl, crawls) into the tent.

▶ Choose two of the verbs you circled. Write a sentence using each verb.

_____

_____

More About Subject/Verb Agreement

► Choose the correct action word from the box to complete each sentence.
Write it on the line.

> If the naming part of a sentence is a noun or pronoun that names one, the verb ends in **-s**, except for the pronouns **I** and **you**. If the naming part is a noun or pronoun that names more than one, the verb does not end in **-s.**

play	run	dive	climb	throw
plays	runs	dives	climbs	throws

1 Mia __plays__ ball with her friends.

2 The children like to __play__ together.

3 Juan __runs__ faster than I do.

4 We __run__ on a track team.

5 Tom and Kara __dive__ into the pool.

6 Mary __dives__ without her goggles.

7 They __climb__ very tall trees.

8 Liz __climbs__ steep mountains.

9 Juan and Mia __throws__ balls.

10 I __Throw__ the ball to Juan.

She hops.

They hop.

More About Subject/Verb Agreement

▶ Fill in the bubble next to the verb that correctly completes the sentence.

1 Bobby _____ a sandwich for lunch.

○ bring   ○ brings

2 Maria _____ rice and black beans.

○ like   ○ likes

3 Bobby and Maria _____ lunches.

○ trade   ○ trades

4 The twins _____ fish sandwiches.

○ eat   ○ eats

5 The children _____ milk with their lunches.

○ drink   ○ drinks

6 They _____ fresh fruit for dessert.

○ buy   ○ buys

7 Jill _____ for a ripe, yellow banana.

○ ask   ○ asks

8 Aki _____ strawberries and blueberries.

○ want   ○ wants

9 Nathan _____ grapes on his tray.

○ put   ○ puts

10 Paulo and Sylvia _____ seats at the table.

○ find   ○ finds

Verbs *have, had*

▶ Read each sentence. Write *have, has,* or *had* on the line in the sentence. Then write *now* or *past* on the line at the end to show if the sentence takes place now or in the past.

> The verb **have** is irregular. Use **have** or **has** to tell about the present. Use **had** to tell about the past.

1 The man _____ many people in his restaurant last week. _____

2 He _____ good food in his kitchen. _____

3 Now the restaurant _____ ten tables. _____

4 The boy _____ time to help his father today. _____

5 The girl _____ time, too. _____

6 The children _____ fun making salads and setting the tables today. _____

7 They _____ a good time together in the restaurant. _____

8 They _____ fun yesterday, too. _____

Verbs *have, had*

► Choose the correct word from the chart to complete each sentence.

The verb **have** is irregular. Use **have** or **has** to tell about the present. Use **had** to tell about the past.

In the Present	In the Past
have, has	had

1 Joe _____ new running shoes.

2 I _____ new shoes, too.

3 Last week we _____ old shoes.

4 I _____ a green shirt on.

5 Joe _____ a blue shirt on.

6 Yesterday we both _____ red shirts on.

7 Last year we _____ to walk to the park.

8 Now, I _____ skates.

9 Now, Joe _____ a bike.

Verbs *have, has, had*

▶ Read each sentence. If the underlined word is correct, fill in the last bubble. If not, fill in the bubble next to the correct word.

1 I <u>have</u> a pet bird.

   ⚬ has   ⚬ had   ⚬ correct as is

2 Now, she <u>had</u> big white wings.

   ⚬ has   ⚬ have   ⚬ correct as is

3 Before, she <u>has</u> little white wings.

   ⚬ have   ⚬ had   ⚬ correct as is

4 The baby bird <u>have</u> closed eyes when it was born.

   ⚬ has   ⚬ had   ⚬ correct as is

5 Now the baby bird <u>had</u> open eyes.

   ⚬ has   ⚬ have   ⚬ correct as is

6 The mother and baby birds <u>had</u> fun now.

   ⚬ has   ⚬ have   ⚬ correct as is

7 The baby bird <u>has</u> little wings now.

   ⚬ have   ⚬ had   ⚬ correct as is

8 It <u>had</u> even smaller wings when it was born.

   ⚬ has   ⚬ have   ⚬ correct as is

Answer Key

Page 4
1. T   3. Q   5. T   7. T
2. Q   4. T   6. Q

Page 5
1. T, .
2. S, .
3. D, ?
4. I, ?
5. M, .
6. Will he take the cat home?

Page 6
1. correct as is   6. When is
2. The vet   7. He has
3. cats.   8. the vet.
4. correct as is   9. goldfish?
5. Do you   10. Will you

Page 7
1. E.   3. E   5. E
2. C   4. E   6. C
7. Be yourself!
8. Don't copy other people.

Page 8
1. fear
2. excitement
3. surprise
4. anger
5. Please don't be upset!
6. Answers will vary.
7. Answers will vary.

Page 9
1. You are a great hopper!
2. The picture looks beautiful!
3. I can paint, too!
4. correct as is
5. Teach me how to hop.
6. Hop backward like this.

Page 10
1. I, .
2. M, I, ?
3. I, !
4. C, I, ?
5. B, I, .
Telling Sentences: I sail my boat in the lake. Bill and I fly the kite.
Questions: May I have a turn? Can Kiku and I play?
Exclamations: I am so happy!

Page 11
1. T   3. T   5. Q   7. Q
2. C   4. C   6. E
8. I, Answers will vary.
9. I, Answers will vary.
10. I, Answers will vary.

Page 12
1. I have fun with my bike.
2. Can I ride to the beach?
3. I find a pretty shell.
4. correct as is
5. Get the shovel.
6. What a mess I made!

Page 13
1. boy, boat
2. brothers, park
3. girl, grandmother
4. boats, lake
5. Friends, needle, thread, sail
People: boy, brothers, girl, grandmother, friends
Places: park, lake
Things: boat, boats, needle, thread, sail

Page 14
Circled nouns: village, office, cane, pencil, doctor, boy, bed, aunt, school
People: doctor, boy, aunt
Places: village, school, office
Things: cane, pencil, bed

Page 15
1. no   4. yes   7. person
2. yes   5. place   8. thing
3. no   6. person

Page 16
1. George Ancona   4. Coney Island
2. Mexico   5. Honduras
3. Jorgito   6. Tio Mario
People: George Ancona, Jorgito, Tio Mario
Places: Mexico, Coney Island, Honduras

Page 17
1. Sue   5. Tonya
2. California   6. Sue Wong
3. Los Angeles   7. Shore Road
4. Pacific Ocean   8. Austin, Texas
Answers will vary.

Page 18
1. person   5. Emilio
2. place   6. Orlando
3. person   7. Disney World
4. place   8. Main Street

Page 19
1. runs   5. misses
2. wears   6. waits
3. smacks   7. writes
4. holds   8. helps

Page 20
1. watch   4. cheers   7. yells
2. throws   5. hits   8. eat
3. opens   6. runs

Page 21
1. action verb
2. not an action verb
3. not an action verb
4. not an action verb
5. action verb
6. action verb
7. not an action verb
8. action verb
9. action verb
10. not an action verb

Page 22
2. Crow, X
3. The water, X
6. One mouse, X

Page 23
1. a. Lin likes to play soccer.
2. b. Her friends watch her play.
3. a. They cheer for Lin.
4. a. Her mom goes to all of her games.
5. a. The coach is very proud of Lin.

Page 24
1. telling part
2. naming part
3. not the whole part
4. not the whole part
5. saw the cat go away
6. Then the bird
7. After a minute, the cat
8. walked back, too

Page 25
1. planted   4. discovered
2. watered   5. (blank)
3. weeded   6. pulled

Page 26
1. pushed   4. followed
2. splashed   5. washed
3. rolled
Answers will vary.

Page 27
1. visited   5. asked
2. correct as is   6. correct as is
3. correct as is   7. correct as is
4. talked   8. showed

Page 28
1. He, Wendell
2. She, Mother
3. They, The pigs
4. it, a board game
5. They, The pigs and Wendell
6. He, Wendell

Page 29
1. it   3. It   5. He
2. They   4. she

Page 30
1. Mrs. Fultz   4. The pigs
2. The boy   5. He
3. The house   6. they

Page 31
Exclamation: What a big mango! This tastes great!
Command: Buy me an avocado. Come over for dinner.
Question: Is that a banana? Did you find the fruit?
Telling Sentence: I want to eat dinner. I like mangoes.

Page 32
1. T   3. T   5. E   7. Q
2. Q   4. C   6. C   8. E

Page 33
1. command   5. exclamation
2. question   6. telling
3. exclamation   7. question
4. command   8. telling

Page 34
1. Two brothers can live together.
2. Hungbu will find a new home.
3. Mother will fix the house.
4. Will Sister clean the house?
5. Can the bird help them?

Page 35
1. Will I find some wood? QUESTION
2. Each of us must help. STATEMENT
3. Where are the trees? QUESTION
4. That is your pumpkin. Is that your pumpkin?
5. You can help cut the pumpkin. Can you help cut the pumpkin?

Page 36
1. Dad made eggs for breakfast.
2. He cracked open four eggs.
3. Do you like eggs?
4. Did you help him?
5. Beat eggs with a fork.
6. correct as is

Page 37
1. accordion(s)
2. brush(es)
3. clock(s), watch(es)
4. flower(s), box(es)
accordions, clocks, flowers brushes, watches, boxes

Page 38
1. sandwiches   5. boxes
2. lunches   6. dresses
3. lunchboxes   7. coats
4. dishes   8. benches

Page 39
1. sketches   5. correct as is
2. correct as is   6. dresses
3. foxes   7. balls
4. correct as is   8. correct as is

Page 40
1. brown, heavy
2. striped, two
3. little, six
4. brown, heavy, striped, little
5. two, six

Page 41
1. zoo, big   3. girls, two
2. giraffe, tall   4. spots, brown
color word: brown
size words: tall, big
number word: two

Page 42
1. red   4. big   7. huge
2. yellow   5. three   8. Two
3. purple   6. little

Page 43
1. is, now   4. is, now
2. are, now   5. am, now
3. were, past   6. was, past

Page 44
1. is/was, one   4. are, more
2. is/was, one   5. was, one
3. were, more   6. are, more

Page 45
1. past, one
2. present, more than one
3. past, more than one
4. past, more than one
5. past, more than one
6. present, one

page 46
1. present   4. present   7. past
2. present   5. past   8. past
3. present   6. past

page 47
1. went   3. does   5. Do
2. goes   4. did   6. go

Page 48
1. goes   4. go   7. went
2. do   5. did   8. did
3. does   6. went

Page 49
1. "Let's go on a picnic."
2. "That's a great idea."
3. "What should we bring?"
4. "We should bring food."
5. "Yes, let's bring lots and lots of food."
6. "You're no help at all!"
7. Answers will vary.

Page 50
1. "It is raining!"
2. "What will we do today?"
3. "We could read."
4. "Maybe the sun will come out soon."
5. "But what will we do now?"
6. "Use your imagination!"
Answers will vary.

Page 51
1. "Let's make a sand castle," said Lenny.
2. "Where's the pail and shovel?" asked Sonya.
3. Sara said, "Maybe Otis can help."
4. "Do you want to dig?" asked Lenny.
5. Sonya shouted, "Get some water!"
6. "Look what we made!" cried the children.

Page 52
1. aren't, are not
2. doesn't, does not
3. can't, cannot
4. couldn't, could not
5. didn't, did not
6. isn't, is not
7. hadn't   had not
8. don't   do not
9. weren't   were not

Page 53
1. couldn't   3. aren't   5. don't
2. wasn't   4. can't   6. didn't
Sentences will vary

Page 54
1. aren't   4. haven't   7. couldn't
2. isn't   5. don't   8. weren't
3. can't   6. didn't

Page 55
1. writes   5. closes   9. call
2. meets   6. forget   10. hear
3. ride   7. locks
4. shop   8. bang

page 56
1. play   5. run   9. sleeps
2. hides   6. stand   10. sleep
3. chase   7. closes
4. calls   8. nudges

Page 57
1. make   5. hang   9. wear
2. cuts   6. buy   10. sell
3. use   7. picks
4. glow   8. picks

Page 58
1. camp   3. walks   5. cook
2. likes   4. build   6. crawl
Sentences will vary.

Page 59
1. plays   5. dive   9. throw
2. play   6. dives   10. throw
3. runs   7. climb
4. run   8. climbs

Page 60
1. brings   5. drink   9. puts
2. likes   6. buy   10. find
3. trade   7. asks
4. eat   8. wants

Page 61
1. had; past   5. has; now
2. had; past   6. have; now
3. has; now   7. have; now
4. has; now   8. had; past

page 62
1. has   4. have   7. had
2. have   5. has   8. have
3. had   6. had   9. has

Page 63
1. correct as is   5. has
2. has   6. have
3. had   7. correct as is
4. had   8. correct as is